Imperfections

seven broken hearts
&
one red balloon

Rui Lima

2018

©

nothing of this world
is mine or yours

we belong far away
from here

maybe
there

the moment
you know
who you are

and
what you need
to be

your true propose
begins

i

wished a hill

but

received

a mountain

i

feel the pain

of climbing

such gift

but

i

am

grateful

the heart hurts

when broken

by the power

of love

or

the weakness

of hate

i
do not do crazy

too crazy
to handle

is

certainly

too crazy
to love

the eternity

of my consciousness

enriches the infinity

of my

realization and existence

i

am

the mystical world

that

i

decided

to

become

never is a long way

from today

....

secrets

are remedies

of brutal

reality

let the rain

bring flowers

and

hide my tears

we mastered love

and

we felt hate

we

laugh and cried

we

existed

together

*Happiness
does not
come alone
where there is
only desire*

i

shaped

happiness

universally

even the shadows

of

unhappiness

transforms

the days

to

uncertain

sadness

play the music
of the gods

and
sit by the fire
completing the puzzle

of
your heart

one by one
created great distance
from themselves and others

i

remain

by my side

i
understand happiness
when
i
feel your smile
and
digest your thoughts

take me

to the moon

and

let me be

i

want to go home

i

want to be free

one red balloon

and

98 others
flew away into the blue sky

we stay
looking at the stars

pondering
when we would depart

all

the imperfections

of the world

are mastered by humanity

and

by our

master

i

desire less than rain

i

seek less than nothing

just because

i

want to endure happiness

one

more time

i

dream of happiness

i

dream of you

so many days passed

and

i

am

still

waiting for you

seven

chess moves

combination

promotion

sacrifice

check

checkmate

attack

?

you

die

our inner selves

are thirsty

for mindful knowledge

knowledge

to be

acknowledged

and

reborn

you make me happy
in the morning
when
the smell of your skin
touches my lips
and
i
purify my thoughts
in your eyes

when
your smile slaves
my hands into your body

and
you
become my ecstasy

my
genuine nature
is to save
is to love
and to care

even
when your nature
is to sting me

earth
does not refuse
seeds

therefore

i

will not refuse

you

create and heal
do not
destroy

remember

you
are not a child

you
are like everyone else
delivering a message
from the universe

the last time

i care this much

i

died

be awake

that
is
what you must be

there is life
after birth

believe

unborn child

i
insist
to love
who hates

and never to hate
who loves

recycle your worries
respect your happiness
eliminate your desires
enjoy enlightenment

you are awake

finally

misery
requires the opposite
of happiness

i

wish

you were happy with me

we are happy
today and tomorrow

because

we

know to be happy
unconditionally

all things
are effects of causes

i
love you

do you love me?

do not judge
never judge

stop judging
based on subjective ideas

the laws of nature
are clear

awareness clarifies
the most foggy
mind

faith

wonder

determination

stay and go

awareness

let

me

tell

you

about

Zen

the ultimate secret
to achieve freedom:

- do not fear death -

the one
free from death
was born
free

my fathers' discipline
made me stronger

good

wiser

fair

and

reasonable

if your goal
is to be free

you must study
the nature
of your
cage

the highest wisdom
breaths attention
and
conquers stillness

change your opinions
surrender your speculations
empty your perceptions

then

know
Zen

the fearless attitude
is spontaneous

i

fear
lack of peace

what do you fear?

a frog knows
how a fly tastes

and
a snake knows
how a frog tastes

we

will be

our future

character

some parents

suffer more than others

and

some people

will never

be

parents

`

but

may suffer

i

was obsessed

about you

we

were fourteen

i

eat everyday
chocolate cheesecake with strawberries

i

am

happy

are you happy?

the voices of nature
speak with me calmly

i

am

at peace

with nature

what brings us together

has more power

than the gods

and

more wisdom

than eternity

what is it?

i

am

accountable

for my actions

and my thoughts

until

i

die

today
nothing matters
more than
the blue sky
reflecting
the rebel waves
of the beach

i
feel sorry
for the broken hearts
drying on the sun
and
the limping star fish

*matilda & max
do not love denny
as much*

i

love you

it is my intention
to seek light

if
darkness returns

the heavy thoughts passed

i

am

again

with peace

the master sculptor
pursues the perfect stone
to sculptor perfection

i

recognize characters
by the sound of their voices

secret tones of envy
when congratulating

and

tones of satisfaction
when condoling

i

also met
sincere voices

i

know the way
to the mountain
of joy

the path is narrow

there is no desire
there is no hatred
there is no worries
there is no suffering

you
may enter
alone

i

am

a dream of a dream

of

something or someone

dreaming of me

who am i?

focus
on enlightenment

everything else
is exact

stop thinking
and
start walking

said the eagle
to the turtle

patience
does not discriminate

apply it

*the world goes
on becoming more beautiful*

*because
of wise efforts
and
less greed*

your tongue has no bone
so you can use it freely

for love

or

for hate

my
heartbeat
is proud of me

i

do not seek

approval or acceptance

from no-one

my

self-realization

is real

we

are the people

practicing the way

and

scrabbling wonders

nothing in the world
is hidden

not even

this or that

i
stay in the now
waiting for the world
to wake up

let me remind you
of the beauty of simplicity

just watch the rain
and the rays of the sun

just feel the sea
and the curves of the wind

just smell the bellis perennis
and touch the earth

just look for you
in what you must be

i

sit in the midst of everything

and

remain stillness

forever

learning everything

that is to know

and

by awaking the status

of curiosity

i

exist

totally

be
genuine in all things

become the best
of you

enjoy
the solitude
and beauty of nature

climb
the highest mountain
you may find

look
at the stars shimmering

understand
the sights
sounds
and smells
and
return home

slowly

set back to comprehend
what you don't understand

you may be too close to see
or too far to acknowledge

set back
again

adjust
to the sun and the rain

like flowers
do

vast emptiness
fulfil enlightenment

not holiness

*the power
to change everything
starts with changing
your attitude*

perception

commands

imagination

your thoughts
are what you are

and

your thoughts
are what you may become

your thoughts
are simply
you

you
are never defeated
by others

only
by yourself

your
clothes do not make you

but

your attitude

do

let me tell you
about happiness
when you find time
to listen

death
may bring us
to a happy place

and

conclude
physical pain

we

were happier

than we are now

we

were young

impulsive

determined

ambitious

and

in

love

i

am happy

eating eggs

and

i

am happy

feeding chickens

happiness
does not seek itself

do

not let

criticism or praise

disturb or distract

your

heart

keep your mind

clear

illusions

blind us

and

rob us

from ourselves

clarify the mind

and

arrive at your source

a calm and settled mind
will achieve enlightenment
under the sun or the moon

meditate

as much
permitted

i
instructed you
to be happy

go with the flow

you
will find
your way out
of the mountain

and
back to the sea

happiness

is appropriate

for everyone

even for you

and

me

imagination
art and philosophy
make me happy
or disappointed

the one

who loves the most

suffers the most

i
loved you enough
to understand
that hate has no chance
to conquer
my feelings

we

unconditionally

love

when we are capable

to care

unconditionally

war and love

may seed

predicaments

to love

is to

exist

everywhere

i
hold the universe
in my mind
as much
you
do

do not seek love
until
you are able to handle
storms
springs
and
dreams

when the heart laughs
the heart fears nothing

the benefits of laugher

are not recognized

by miserable people

time is shortened

by age

and

time

determines

my existence

time is an illusion

how much illusion

do you have?

free are the birds
with flying wings

and

no cage

an hour and a second
are from the same time

sometimes

seven broken hearts
drying under the sun

wolves eating hay
lambs running

one red balloon
is forever
gone

i

am

in peace

genuine freedom

is enough

today

triskele
triskelion

birth
death
rebirth

mystery and promise
a moment on a wheel turns
turns and turns

how much fear would you have
after knowing eternity?